WE WILL BE FINE

Rowan Lyster is a poet and physiotherapist from Herefordshire, based in Bristol. Her poems have been widely published in journals including *Magma*, *Poetry Wales* and *The Rialto*, have placed in competitions and been commissioned by the Southbank Centre. She is a member of the Southbank Centre New Poets' Collective 2022-23.

First published in 2025 by Little Betty, an imprint of Bad Betty Press
Cobden Place, Cobden Chambers, Nottingham NG1 2ED

badbettypress.com

Copyright © Rowan Lyster 2025

Rowan Lyster has asserted her right to be identified as the author of this work in accordance with Section 77 of the Copyright, Designs and Patents Act of 1988.

PB ISBN: 978-1-913268-84-8
EPUB ISBN: 978-1-913268-85-5

A CIP record of this book is available from the British Library.

Book design by Amy Acre

We Will Be Fine

ROWAN LYSTER

For SWC

LITTLE BETTY

CONTENTS

Stop Motion	7
I'm not surprised that it's warm out	8
Getting stuck in the rain	9
We are all very sad and very worried	10
I've fallen for yet another	11
If you feel yourself disintegrating	12
Naked mole rats	13
When you saw me flying you couldn't take your eyes off me	14
Butternut soup	15
Adults	16
Ant societies have division of labour	17
In the night while you were sleeping	18
Mind control	19
Stay	20
Nothing was good enough	22
Eventually	23
Preoccupied by a sense that you may be unhappy	24
There aren't many people I'd give a kidney for	25
Outside the window	26
Sardines on toast	27
a bad summer	28
Let's walk around the cemetery until you're someone else	29
Acknowledgements	30

STOP MOTION

Please World let me be
the person saying no
instead of the one asking
will you be my friend
on the last tube to Morden,
mascara beetling down my cheeks.
I'll do something nice
another time. I'm busy
googling how to meet people,
wondering why my stomach
is full of wasps.
These days I'm the healthiest
I've ever been. I run weekly.
When I notice imperfections
in someone else's relationship,
I write them down in a notebook.
When I go to a wedding,
I make models of the happy couple,
move the little plasticine arms
until they snap. A shutter sounds
each time the scene changes.
In the next frame
I will be the hero.

I'M NOT SURPRISED THAT IT'S WARM OUT

I'm just so busy it's illegal
to have a hole inside
dragging it round on picnics and dates
trying to give something I love away
my very best smile
a terrible kick
from knowing everything like a saint
demons never startle me
I am cold and viscous for safety reasons
stay within reach of the fire blanket

GETTING STUCK IN THE RAIN

seeking shelter on the church porch –
give it five hours and the two of you
are newlyweds expecting your first,
rebuilding this derelict cottage you've found.
The best way to learn to juggle is stand
against a wall. That way you can't accidentally
step back. Why not start with swords?
You're looking radiant – your swollen body,
your manicured hands grabbing at air.

WE ARE ALL VERY SAD AND VERY WORRIED

Boxes from three moves ago accumulate
the moment we pause. Another line
on the to do list. We have made a rota
for our interactions and too much overlap
nauseates us, like a stranger's sweat. Perhaps
we're at the point where the DJ ought to play
Mr Brightside, only we are far too busy
wiping our garden fences with J-Cloths
to scream along. Now it's not enough
to go to the shops for vitamins, despite
what the bus-stop posters claim. Let's spend
all night pressed against the glass.

I'VE FALLEN FOR YET ANOTHER

boy who is locked in a box
which is inside a bigger box
inside a lead-lined coffer
at the bottom of the ocean
in a shark infested area
wrists and ankles bound with
a whole roll of duct tape
I am uncertain if the boy
has done this to himself
or if it was done to him
but whichever is the case
every move of his seems
much more exciting than
if those hands were free
to make any kind of effort

IF YOU FEEL YOURSELF DISINTEGRATING

closely examine the grout
between platform tiles   follow
the line   with your finger
if it helps
      crawl
beneath the flow of   always the same faces
the woman peeling extinction rebellion stickers
off the floor   is she collecting them

you have observed   these
      or other similar faces   before
because   as you have noticed
all the faces   have been used up

passengers
      are reminded
it is extremely important
to breathe
    not just once

but again   & again

NAKED MOLE-RATS

I went to the zoo instead of work, and looked at naked mole-rats.
The display was written in first person, as if by the naked mole-rats.
They spoke about the social and sexual structures of naked mole-rats
in their colonies, explaining that the queen of the naked mole-rats
is thought to emit a pheromone preventing other naked mole-rats
from sexually maturing, so they remain adolescent naked mole-rats.
I don't know if you're interested in the proclivities of naked mole-rats.
When you ask what's on my mind, I don't mention naked mole-rats
and once we've both had a few I barely consider naked mole-rats
but when we remove our clothes, I can't stop seeing naked mole-rats.

WHEN YOU SAW ME FLYING YOU COULDN'T TAKE YOUR EYES OFF ME

None of the other girls can fly.
Not even her.
I chose my moment carefully.
Waited until you happened to glance at the skyline,
then I did a big swoop.
You gaped.
I said "Oh hi"
as I landed just below you.
You put your book on the grass,
one eyebrow cocked.
That was when I knew.
We spoke for a while.
Not about flying.
I caught you scanning my shoulders,
trying to catch a glimpse of my back.
As they say in magazines,
don't make it too easy.
Before you had a chance to ask,
I took off again.
After that it was a matter of time.
All the pain had been worthwhile.

BUTTERNUT SOUP

when the squash gives way its belly
splits wide stinks like a warning
like parsnips and grass
can persuasion take place without heat
cayenne cumin handfuls of garlic
lightly crushed beneath a blade
tip bright lumps in the food waste caddy
allow the pulp time to break down
with enough paprika you'll barely taste it
onions are waiting in the pan

ADULTS

Half the women in my choir have babies
and the other half are freezing their eggs.
We coo at the babies and smile wide,
hoping no one will notice our terror.
Half the women in my choir are pregnant,
and all of us are babies. We wail in chorus,
hoping someone will check what we need.
We're hungry, we scream. We're all alone,
packed into our solitude like piglets.
Half the women are full of futures
and the rest of us are already too late.
Our eggs chatter among themselves
about geriatric mothers and wage gaps.
Don't worry, exclaim the men, there's
no freedom under capitalism anyway!
When we begin breathing together
our bellies swell. I wish this would stop,
we cry, while feeling quietly thrilled
that we now contain two skeletons.

ANT SOCIETIES HAVE DIVISION OF LABOUR

approximately one million ants per human on earth you're grinning social ants cooperate if you notice my finger tapping you don't show it some are regarded as invasive the table crawls unwashed dishes establishing themselves where they have been introduced between us now I can't unsee it to support the colony I twitch your hand off my shoulder a crushed ant emits an alarm pheromone I wipe the counter into an attack frenzy ants on the chopping board survive efforts to eradicate the sounds of your chewing their acts of suicidal altruism the will to carry crumbs away

IN THE NIGHT WHILE YOU ARE SLEEPING

I offer you the apple I can feel through my pillow
you roll further away so I have to keep it

my teeth won't go through the skin
but I think perhaps I can swallow it whole

it's hard to breathe past the apple
lodged between my tongue and palate

you can't hear my muffled voice
as I become all apple my eyes filling solid

everything turning waxy and red-green
October rain rounding my limbs

into my body and I wonder
will you be into me tomorrow

when you wake to find me nothing
but fraying stalk and bruised flesh

I hope you will still want to hold me
in the palm of your hand please

polish me against your jacket
and carry me in your pocket all day

MIND CONTROL

I suspect the trees
aren't real. Grass
creaks. I must
sit here carefully
to avoid being
seen. The air
is fraying. The backs
of my knees itch.
Though these leaves
are convincing.
Small warty bumps.
Insect holes. I am
entirely still except
a muscle below
my left eye. The ducks
are pretending
to be ducks.
The first time I
saw my own blood
I did not believe it
was part of me—
too bright.

STAY

I would never ask you for anything. In my garden, I have buried
a piece of stone, which I took from your garden. I know it won't
grow by itself but I like to know it's there. Before the neighbours wake,
I creep outside to check if the stone has developed into anything new.
It is always just a stone, buried. I wonder if you look out of the window
and think, something is missing in that corner, but can't quite put your finger
on what. If you ever asked, I would give the stone back without question.

★

All your herbs are dying and there is nothing I can do to fix them.
Perhaps you shouldn't have planted the basil. The climate here is wrong
for basil, but I watched you plant it anyway. Now even the hardiest shrubs
are suffering from something unnamed. You tend them all day, weeping
over brittle black sticks of rosemary. The oregano is diminishing, a leaf
dropping on the ground, then another. You wrap stalks in cotton wool.
You must know it's hopeless, yet you continue patting the soil.

*

I have taken your garden and it is ours now. I moved it piece by piece, using the tools I had to hand, reassembled it as close to the original as I could manage. See how the path curves at the exact same point? I can't bear to watch you crying like that. You are still welcome here, truly I'd love to see you thriving. Come and sit with me on the bench over by the wall. It can be our bench. I'm sure the plants will begin to flourish, if only the sun would come back.

*

Something has budded from the stone I planted. A long blue flower. I am afraid to look in case you are sat in its trumpet, cross-legged. If I were to bury my face in the flower, no one would ever see me but you. I know you won't be happy with this arrangement. You'll want to see other people as well as me. You'll want to see others instead of me, even though we've got to know each other so well. I won't look at your face, lit blue through the petals. That way, you can't tell me to go.

NOTHING WAS GOOD ENOUGH

I looked it in the mouth and saw points of light in all colours imaginable, stretching back in its palate for miles. I said *you shouldn't have*. You agreed. I wracked my brain for weeks about what to give you in return. For a while I considered taking all your problems and making them mine, but you might have missed them. Anyway, I didn't want you to think of me in just a practical way. In the end I decided to give you back the horse, inside out, so you could see its beauty all the time. I plunged my hands in its warm middle. It felt like pondweed in the sun. When I returned the horse to you, it was a mass of pulp, the lights from within a little smeared. You thanked me but wouldn't look me in the eye. If only you knew how long it took.

EVENTUALLY

We reached a cliff
over which a family had just disappeared.

We knew what was going on and turned back
between the stones of the ruined chapel.

You picked a berry and asked if I wanted one.
I waited to see if something bad would happen.

A cloud snuck up and took away the landscape.
You had grown a long white beard.

You wrapped your left foot in my scarf and said
if the rest of you froze I'd have something to take home.

I made a replica of you from grass
and ate it when you were looking away.

You told me you were planning to retrain as a weather god
which might mean leaving town for a while.

On the way down we met ourselves coming up.
We smiled at each other as we passed.

They smiled because they were still new
and we smiled because the hard bit was over.

PREOCCUPIED BY A SENSE
THAT YOU MAY BE UNHAPPY

I suggest a fun night out, in which we will visit
and destroy a series of homes. It seems proper
to begin with the mansion, which, naturally,
we burn down. From below the ha-ha,
we watch inhabitants flee in dressing gowns.
Despite the flames reflected in your eyes,
you lack a certain zeal. We move on
to more conceptual methods:
ant eggs in the curtain linings,
floodlights installed outside bedroom windows,
sinister messages daubed on walls.
We deal with colleagues, and then friends.
You sleep with someone's husband;
I steal a newborn and exchange it for a cabbage.
Our family homes are less of a challenge.
Through the letterbox, a manila envelope
containing a warning note and new passports.
At dawn, when nobody else is left,
you bundle yourself into a cupboard,
duct-tape your own mouth and ankles
while I take a clawhammer to the fuse box,
block the sink and leave the taps running,
hoping it might put a smile on your face.

THERE AREN'T MANY PEOPLE I'D GIVE A KIDNEY FOR

You could have become one of them.
We can both taste that third White Russian
thick on your breath. If I knew how to ask,
you'd clean your teeth for me lickety split
but there are damp patches on your polo shirt
and I wish you would stop mentioning skin.
Your eyelashes are beautiful, I'm only sorry
I don't want to be near them any more.
As long as the truth stays out of the room,
no one will get hurt. Isn't that true?
Hand me a mallet; I'll take it to your legs
or mine, to avoid the need to mention
that ten-pack of Durex in its plastic seal,
waiting intact on your bathroom floor.

OUTSIDE THE WINDOW

the daisies are moving on
and the trees on the hilltop care so little
they have faded
from green to pale blue.
The drying hay is indifferent to you
and the birds
are busy with their own lives.
Even the fence
is just getting on
with separating one place
from the next,
never once glancing back
at the milk bottle of flowers
on the windowsill
which without their roots
are bound to die soon.

SARDINES ON TOAST

I peel open the can and glance
towards the window in case
you decide to turn up
the bodies are pressed
together glistening in oil
half listening for your car over
the bassline I sway
as I angle the tin carefully
pretend to watch the liquid escape
sing along *my heart just dropped*
thinking about you I take a fork
crush spines and fins and flesh
onto burnt edges *the world just stops*
when I'm without you a squeeze
of lemon some pepper snare
ticking like held breath I turn on
the grill through the glass
you're taking off your jumper
a glimpse of your skin
the fire alarm screams

A BAD SUMMER

this year has healed over
smooth and new   almost
the same shape as before and
we will be fine if we don't think
about all those fingers gone missing
surely due to resurface
soon
        blossoming like
mushroom caps   the end
of something bright against clay
or where the hedge
dissects the sky   look
among shattered hazel
a wrist

LET'S WALK AROUND THE CEMETERY UNTIL YOU'RE SOMEONE ELSE

You can tell me you finally know what to do with your life.
You'll forget your lunch; I'll share. Each gravestone on the long avenue
will bear our names against different dates. Beloved husband.
And our children. Two, three? Maybe more – maybe infants,
depending on the century. Sadly missed. We'll put down peonies
we've chosen at the florist, lay them gently on the compressing soil.
You'll be eloquent. *Forever in our thoughts.* I'll cry behind your back.
Your jumper will have more holes than before, but will fit your shoulders
the way it used to. Under the mask I'll know you're smiling.
In the blackthorn I might spot a jay, wings a flash of implausible blue.
Each time we turn a corner, our hands won't touch.

ACKNOWLEDGEMENTS

Many thanks to the editors of the following journals in which versions of some of these poems have appeared: *14 Magazine*, *Anthropocene*, *Bath Magg*, *Iamb*, *Gutter*, *Magma*, *Mslexia*, *Poetry Wales*, *Tentacular*, *The Four Faced Liar* and *Under The Radar*. The poem 'Sardines on Toast' (p27) includes found text from the song 'Fire for You' by Cannons.

I am grateful to all the writers, tutors and organisations who have shaped my writing over the years, and to everyone in the wonderful collectives who have supported me and helped hone some of these poems: the Crocodile Collective, the Foxglove Collective, the Southbank Centre New Poets' Collective 2022-23, and Somerville Writers' Club (where it all started).

Enormous thanks to Oliver Fox whose generous reading of this manuscript made it sharper and better. Thank you to everyone at Little Betty for being a dream publisher in all respects, and particularly to Vanessa Kisuule not just for being a conscientious and encouraging editor, but also for always pushing these poems to be more unhinged.

Thanks, and love, to my family and to Kieran.

www.ingramcontent.com/pod-product-compliance
Lightning Source LLC
Chambersburg PA
CBHW021639080526
44584CB00015BA/1607